MAR   2009

A+
books

Where Words

In and Out

by Tami Johnson

Capstone
press

Mankato, Minnesota

A+ Books are published by Capstone Press,
151 Good Counsel Drive, P.O. Box 669, Mankato, Minnesota 56002.
www.capstonepress.com

1 2 3 4 5 6 12 11 10 09 08 07

Library of Congress Cataloging-in-Publication Data
Johnson, Tami.
    In and out / by Tami Johnson.
        p. cm.—(A+ books. Where words)
    Summary: "Simple text and color photographs introduce the basic concept of in and out"—Provided
by publisher.
    Includes bibliographical references and index.
    ISBN-13: 978-0-7368-6733-7 (hardcover)
    ISBN-10: 0-7368-6733-3 (hardcover)
    ISBN-13: 978-0-7368-7851-7 (softcover pbk.)
    ISBN-10: 0-7368-7851-3 (softcover pbk.)
    1. Space perception—Juvenile literature. I. Title. II. Series.
BF469.J65 2007
153.7'52—dc22   2006022808

Credits

Megan Schoeneberger, editor; Juliette Peters, designer; Charlene Deyle, photo researcher; Scott
    Thoms, photo editor

Photo Credits

Capstone Press/Karon Dubke, 4–5, 6, 14, 15, 16, 17
Corbis/Barbara Peacock, 23; Bruce Burkhardt, 29 (top); Carl & Ann Purcell, 29 (middle);
    W. Perry Conway, 13; Wally McNamee, 29 (bottom); zefa/Joson, 26–27
Digital Vision, 20, 21
Dwight R. Kuhn, 8, 9, 10, 11
Getty Images Inc./Iconica/Blue Line Pictures, 25; Iconica/Eric Meola, 12; The Image Bank/Ian
    Royd, cover; Photonica/Doug Plummer, 7; Photonica/GK & Vikki Hart, 18; Taxi/Bay Hippisley,
    24; Taxi/Ryan McVay, 22
Peter Arnold Inc./David Cavagnaro, 28 (top); Lynn Rogers, 28 (middle)
Shutterstock/Troy Casswell, 28 (bottom)
SuperStock/age fotostock, 19

Note to Parents, Teachers, and Librarians

Where Words uses color photographs and a nonfiction format to introduce readers to the vocabulary of space. *In and Out* is designed to be read aloud to a pre-reader, or to be read independently by an early reader. Images and activities encourage mathematical thinking in early readers and listeners. The book encourages further learning by including the following sections: Table of Contents, Fun Facts, Glossary, Read More, Internet Sites, and Index. Early readers may need assistance using these features.

Table of Contents

What Is In? What Is Out?

In is inside of something.
Out is outside of something.

The girl is in the house.
The boy is out of the house.

When we're in, it's fun to look out.

When we're out, it's fun to look in.

A hungry alligator hides in the water waiting quietly, patiently.

Snap! Quick as a flash he pops out of the water to catch a tasty meal.

A baby duck starts its life
in an egg.

Crack! A duckling pecks away at the shell to get out.

Bears stand in the water to catch fish to eat.

Out of the water, bears hunt for tasty berries.

Food In and Out

Milk splashes in the glass.

Oops! Someone spilled all the milk out.

Cookie dough goes in the oven
soft and gooey.

Cookies come out of the oven
smelling oh so good.

Bread goes in the toaster
white and soft.

It comes out of the
toaster brown and crispy.

People In and Out

Soapy bubbles in the tub
get you clean.

When you get out of the tub,
a warm towel feels good.

A big smile shows off the
teeth in your mouth.

If one falls out, don't worry. A new one will soon fill the gap.

The sand in the bucket is just sand.

But when you dump it out,
you can make a sandcastle!

Aaaah! Floating in a cool pool gets you out of the summer heat.

In and Out Facts

When a butterfly comes out of a cocoon, its wings are wet. The butterfly hangs upside down while its wings dry.

Grizzly bears go in caves or dens to hibernate. They sleep through the cold winter months and wake up in springtime.

Lobsters don't have skeletons in their bodies like people do. Instead, the lobster's skeleton is on the outside of its body.

Your first set of teeth has 20 teeth. After your teeth fall out, new ones come in. When you're an adult, you'll have 32 teeth in your mouth.

Here's a different kind of in. Hotels in the country are often called inns.

Here's a different kind of out. In baseball and softball, the umpire decides if a runner is safe or out.

Glossary

alligator (AL-i-gay-tuhr)—a large animal with strong jaws and very sharp teeth

cocoon (kuh-KOON)—a covering of silky threads made by some animals to protect themselves or their eggs

dough (DOH)—a thick, sticky mixture used to make cookies, bread, and muffins

grizzly bear (GRIZ-lee BAIR)—a large brown or gray bear of western North America

hibernate (HYE-bur-nate)—to spend winter in a deep sleep; animals hibernate to survive low temperatures and lack of food.

lobster (LOB-stur)—a sea animal with a hard shell and five pairs of legs

sandcastle (SAND-kass-uhl)—a sculpture made of sand and water that looks like a tiny building or castle

skeleton (SKEL-uh-tuhn)—the bones that support and protect the body of a human or other animal

Read More

Emigh, Karen. *Herman's Hiding Places: Discovering Up, In, Under and Behind.* Arlington, Texas: Future Horizons, 2004.

Johnson, Tami. *Up and Down.* Where Words. Mankato, Minn.: Capstone Press, 2007.

Pearson, Debora. *Kids Do, Animals Too: A Book of Playground Opposites.* New York: Annick Press, 2005.

Internet Sites

FactHound offers a safe, fun way to find Internet sites related to this book. All of the sites on FactHound have been researched by our staff.

Here's how:

1. Visit *www.facthound.com*

2. Choose your grade level.

3. Type in this book ID **0736867333** for age-appropriate sites. You may also browse subjects by clicking on letters, or by clicking on pictures and words.

4. Click on the **Fetch It** button.

FactHound will fetch the best sites for you!

Index